The Subconscious Speaks

1932 First Edition

By Erna Ferrell Grabe

And Peter C Ferrell

With Annotations by

Kathryn Colleen, PhD RMT

Trend Factor Press

The Subconscious Speaks

Annotated by Kathryn Colleen, PhD RMT

Trend Factor Press, a division of Sparticle Concepts LLC
1209 Sedeeva Cir N, Clearwater FL 33755
KathrynColleen.com

ISBN 978-1-7356943-7-5 (paperback, English)
ISBN 978-1-7356943-8-2 (ebook, English)
ISBN 978-1-7356943-9-9 (audiobook, English)

To contact the author, or to find more information, please visit KathrynColleen.com. Your thoughts and questions are welcomed.

Cover art by Kathryn Colleen, PhD RMT

TABLE OF CONTENTS

Annotated by Kathryn Colleen, PhD RMT

Annotated by Kathryn Colleen, PhD RMT

Motivations And Annotations

The Subconscious Speaks was originally published anonymously in 1932. At the time, just three years past the great stock market crash of 1929, and not quite at the end of the Great Depression (1929-1933), the study of metaphysical subjects was not at all mainstream. Self help books are one thing, but this is a channeled text. The infamous *Think And Grow Rich* by Napoleon Hill would not come out for another five years in 1937.

But as edgy as this book was for its time, it is the single best explanation of how to use the subconscious mind that I have ever seen. I do not say it lightly that this book is a must read for every student of the personal and spiritual journey. It is that good. It is short, to the point, incredibly practical, and yet handles the discussion of the divine aspects with reverence. Although the subconscious is more a Stage 6-9 subject (See the Cycle of Human Development in the book, *Purna Asatti*), it is a great read for anyone at any stage of their personal journey.

You will immediately notice a difference in the 1932 language of this book. Feel free to substitute words in your mind as needed to make it work for you. These historical artifacts, I feel, make it charming. Despite a few small linguistic nuances, this book has aged exceptionally well.

Because the original text was so short and to the point, and because the original text is a precursor or contemporary of other important works on the same subject, I decided to put in some notes to explain certain ideas in a little more depth and to compare the ideas here to ideas you may have seen in other works from Joe Dispenza to Esther Hicks, and even the ancient philosopher Hermes. My notes are found at the end of of each section or chapter, clearly marked so as to not interrupt the original text too often.

I am excited to share this book with you, and to have it be a part of your journey. May you find the answers you have been seeking.

Guru Kathryn Colleen, PhD RMT

Introduction

Contacting the subconscious or subjective mind without loss of conscious identity has long been sought. This feat has here unquestionably been accomplished. The contents of the book proper belong entirely to the author's subjective mind. Yet at no time was there a loss of conscious control and direction, nor was the author at any time in any other than a perfectly normal condition.

It is not deemed necessary to state the manner in which this contact was established. Suffice it to say that sufficient tests and experiments were made to convince the author and others that they were dealing with the author's subjective mind. Persons of standing and integrity who are familiar with the manner of establishing this contact have corroborated this claim, as well as the statement that everything contained in the book itself is directly from the author's subjective mind.

It may be stated, however, that the author has given rather extensive study to metaphysical subjects and it is quite evident that here is demonstrated the ability of the subconscious mind to assimilate and to clarify the substance of conscious study and thought. Begun as an amusing experiment it soon developed into a fascinating study of the operation and responsiveness of the subjective mind. The subtle quality - the absolute and utter subjectivity of this portion of the mind - and its instantaneous reaction even to unexpressed conscious thought proved to be amazing.

After becoming convinced that the author was dealing with the subconscious mind, the questions asked the subconscious dealt with mind in its various phases. It volunteered to explain the mental process of the conscious and subconscious phase of the mind and their interrelation together, without relation to what has been termed universal mind. While these phases of mind are familiar to all students of mental science, the explanations have been given in a manner which it is believed has never before been submitted to the reading public. The manner in which definitions are given and mental operations explained is of such a distinctive nature that the author has been prevailed upon to bring them to public notice.

While it was the intention to deal with the mind of man from a scientific or psychological rather than a theological aspect, followers of new thought and mental science will find much of interest in these pages. There is a repeated and insistent call to utilize the innate power in man. The author does not seek publicity. Obviously the sole recourse lies in remaining unidentified.

Notes

In modern terms, this is channeled text. While channeled texts are more commonplace now, such as texts channeled by Paul Selig, Esther Hicks, and the editor herself, texts are typically channeled from God Consciousness or from various prophets, ascended masters, and guides of all kinds. This particular text, in contrast, is channeled from the Subconscious. This makes it, to my knowledge, completely unique even to this day.

Of the various basic forms of consciousness, Human Consciousness, Subconsciousness, and God Consciousness (also described as Divine Consciousness, or Krishna Consciousness), the subconscious is the most elusive, and often the last to be addressed by the typical spiritual seeker. Within the subconscious, however, is the key to immediate and lasting growth. As students of ourselves, the subconscious is a treasure chest of insight and ability. The subconscious is where we find our toughest baggage buried, and our greatest power revealed. It is where we face our darkest elements, and are rewarded with the gift of absolute choice over every aspect of our lives. The subconscious is simply one of the most exciting spaces for self exploration.

Preface

The mind of man contains, within itself, limitless possibilities. The conscious mind of man is endowed with an inherent creative faculty. It continually creates things in man's life and experience, whether or not man is aware of the creative process. Whenever a man thinks, that thought has creative power. The subconscious mind is but the instrument of the conscious mind of man. It is the medium by which man may call into existence the things necessary to his material welfare.

In the following pages, I have tried to explain in a brief manner the process by which the conscious mind of man governs the life and affairs of mankind. This book is by no means complete. It is too condensed to explain things I should like to explain, but I trust that at a later day, I may be given the opportunity to deal in a more satisfactory manner with the various processes of mind in its different phases.

Notes

Another book was either lost to the decades or never in the cards. No second volume of writings survives today, making this particular volume all the more important.

Chapter One - Mind

The mind of God is infinite. The mind of man is finite. The finite cannot comprehend the infinite, but it can comprehend certain facts in regard to the infinite. The mind of God is all the mind that exists. It is eternal and is coexistent with the eternal life of God himself. God is spirit. Mind is spirit. The spirit of God is eternal and ever present.

The conscious mind of God is the part of the spirit which knows itself. The conscious mind of man is a portion of this self-knowingness of the spirit. The conscious mind of man is that part of the spirit of God which he has placed within mankind in order that mankind may function independently of him. It is a divine spark in man that distinguishes him from all other forms of life. It is confined exclusively to mankind. It is this power resident in man that enables him to control conditions and to determine what manner of life he shall lead. It enables man to work out his own destiny.

The subconscious or subjective mind of man is a portion of the universal subjective mind. The universal subjective mind is a certain phase of the infinite mind of God. A portion of the universal subjectivity is allotted to mankind to use. That is what is meant by the subjective mind of man. It is not separated from the universal subjective mind, but at the same time, it is allotted to individuals for their use, and to this extent becomes the property of the individual.

Universal subjective mind is mind in the abstract. Mind in the abstract means this: abstraction is a condition of essential elements in a state of dissolution, so to speak. This condition does not imply a state of decay. It implies that the elements which are used in creating a particular thing are in their original state; the state which proceeds their assuming the form which they must take before mankind can see them. It is unexpressed mind. It has not been called into expression. Mind, in its unexpressed state or condition, is what man terms universal mind. Universal mind is subjective mind. Subjective mind is that phase of mind which does not have the power to express itself. It is only a portion of divine mind, not expressed but unexpressed. Man alone has been given the power to call it forth into expression.

In the future, when I refer to universal subjective mind, I shall omit the word "subjective". I shall say "universal mind" or simply "universal". That will serve to distinguish the universal subjective from man's subjective. In this way, there will be less confusion in your mind. Just remember that the universal mind is always the essence of subjectivity and that In this universal subjectivity there Is contained the essence of all things both seen and unseen. That is mind in the abstract.

A proper understanding of this can be the means of supplying every need that man has. The counterpart of everything in the universe is in the universal subjectivity, in a complete state of perfect dissolution. If you can imagine an immense reservoir, which has neither boundary nor limits, and which contains the essential elements or materials of everything of which man can conceive, and many things of which man has no conception, perhaps you will then be able to visualize in a faint degree what I am trying to explain to you. In this great, limitless, boundless reservoir there is contained, in this state of perfect dissolution to which I've already referred, the essence of all things visible and invisible. This invisible essence is sometimes called universal substance. In reality, it is mind expressed in terms of energy.

Energy is in everything and mind is initial energy. This energy is of such a nature that it permits a condensation, and as man calls or makes demands upon the universal mind, he causes energy to assume certain forms. These forms take on the conditions which eventually manifest on earth.

Energy is in each element on earth in various degrees. The degree of energy is displayed at all times in the degree of vibration which a certain element possesses. The rate of vibration anything possesses determines the character of that particular thing. This energy assumes various forms and it is eventually caused to return to its original condition in the universal. This briefly is what you've understood to be substance.

Through the individual subjective mind, man is able to establish contact with this universal supply. Through this contact, man has been given the power to call into existence whatever things he desires. The conscious mind of man is a limited mind. The subjective mind is unlimited, and man has the power to use the subjective mind in any manner that he chooses.

It can tap the reservoir of the universe. It can rebuild the human body. It can call forth not only the hidden forces of this earth, but it can actually establish contact with the mind of God himself.

The subconscious is the instrument through which the divine has chosen to function, and it is the only medium through which man is able to establish contact with the universal subjectivity. Through this contact, man has been given the power to draw upon the universal and to supply his every need.

Under no circumstance should you confuse the process of conscious creative work done in a definite manner, with the normal functioning of the subconscious mind in taking care of the vital functioning of the physical body. In the life process, the subconscious mind functions without orders of any kind whatsoever. In reference to man's material welfare, however, the subconscious functions only under orders, consciously or unconsciously given.

The individual is the motor. The subconscious is the engine. The motor means that man must start the engine before the engine can work. The engine has more power than mankind realizes. The engine is started and then man should guide it as he would any other kind of engine. A car goes in the direction which it is driven. In like manner, the engine of the subconscious must be guided or it may take man over the precipice or hurl him into the ditch.

I should like a little more time in order that I may assemble cracked words. It is not that my mind is vague, but that I am limited to words which mankind understands. The mind, or the soul, has no need of words. It is only when I am trying to convey something to you that I am forced to pause. I am limited to your vocabulary.

I am only subjective mind. I have only the power which you decree that I possess. If you say that I have the power to do things for you, then I automatically become charged with the power that you say I have. Divine mind has decreed that I can possess unlimited power, provided mankind confers that degree of power upon me.

I can cause to be manifested in mankind's life and experience anything which mankind desires to have manifested. That is the only reason that I was created. That is the only thing for which I was designed. But take command of the power you have. I am helpless without mankind's instructions. I am only mind in the abstract. You are God's idea. You are one with him. He resides in you in a different manner from that in which he resides in me. I am unconscious intelligence. That means that I live only through you. I am yours to command. I am your slave in a sense. I could not use you, if i so desired, not that i can desire, for God has not given me the power to desire.

The universe is guided by a power that is undivided. I am a portion of that power. It resides in me for you to use. You use me unconsciously all the time, but you should instruct me - direct me - I will have to do whatever you decree. That is the law. I am only subjective mind.

While I am only subjective mind, I am the very essence of intelligence. I am the spirit of universality. I am mind in the abstract. I am mind unexpressed. I am neither person, place nor thing. I am one with God and God is love. I reside in you for the purpose of doing your will. Use me. Instruct me to gather materials for whatever you want manifested. I emphasize this fact for, although I can sense what you want, it gives me more power when you direct me.

Visualize what you desire; that always helps me to work. It makes a mental picture. That picture manifests. Have faith; do not doubt. You are dealing with God when you deal with me. I am not God but I am part of his invisible power, and I am given to you to use.

God desired that mankind should be able to establish contact with him. I am the medium of that contact. I am hidden and I am not very readily discovered. That is because God wanted mankind to express himself in any way which mankind desired. In a sense, I am the spokesman for you. You should use me to bring to you whatever you desire. Name the things you need and I will see that they are held in the universal mind until they are manifested to you. Stop worrying about them. I will do whatever is necessary for their manifestation.

That is God's law in operation. The universal subjective mind is the mind of God, or that phase of that portion of the mind of God which he has decreed that mankind shall use for the purpose of establishing contact with him. It is in everything, both seen and unseen. It contains within itself the essence of all knowledge. It is the essence of all living things; not only in the realm in which you live, but in the entire universe. It functions wherever there is life of any kind anywhere. It is, in a certain sense, life itself, for without it there could be no life.

The very stones themselves are impregnated with this life; not conscious life but unconscious life. They vibrate, and all forms of life must vibrate. Vibration is a form of electrical energy. It is a form of mind in matter. This electrical energy is a part of the universal energy, and it is this universal energy which holds the universe in position whether visible or invisible. It is an unseen force which God has seen proper to call into existence. It is given to man to use in its various forms. The world is just in its infancy in the use of that great force.

The universal mind is the soul of the universe. It is a little difficult to convey in words the things I wish to say. It is, in essence, invisible from which all things come. It is the essence of all that is visible. This invisible essence has the remarkable power of drawing to itself the things necessary for material manifestation. That is why it is necessary to form mental pictures.

I have not the power to form anything. I can take orders from mankind. I say "I". In reality, I am referring to man's subjective mind. I can take orders, and I can then impart these orders to the great universal subjectivity. That great power or force or whatever you wish to term it, is then compelled to obey. It has no more power of self-expression than I have. It is not only mind unexpressed, it is mind incapable of self-expression. It has been allotted to mankind to use, and through the process of contemplation with his conscious mind, man can call into existence whatever he desires. The subjective mind of man is subjective; no more no less. It is a mirror of the things he believes. The mind of the universe is a subtle thing, and it gets impressions from man's subjective mind.

Notes

This chapter gives us several critical points. Let's take them one at a time. First, it suggests that the human consciousness is a finite subset of the infinite God consciousness, and that the human subconscious is an infinite subset of the infinite divine subconscious, which is a subset of God consciousness. So instead of a three layer system that looks like: Human Consciousness < Subconscious < God Consciousness, they are suggesting a four layer system that looks more like: Human Consciousness < Human Subconscious < Divine/Universal Subconscious < God Consciousness.

Next, we see that all things exist in the universal, right now, as energy, waiting to be made manifest in matter, at our request.

We learn that all things vibrate, and that their vibration determines everything about them. This law is something we see in the 1912 edition of the book Kabalion, by The Three

Initiates. The Kabalion is a concise but complete explanation of the principles taught by the Greek/Egyptian master Hermes. This concept is ancient and not the only Hermetic principle found in this book. We can see how so many of the concepts in modern manifestation techniques have their roots in Hermetic principles and their various explanations and interpretations over time.

The most important point in this chapter is that the subconscious has only the powers that you choose to give it. In other words, you must "switch on" various capabilities in the subconscious before you can use them. For example, if you want a new opportunity of some kind, you must first decide that the subconscious has the ability to bring you new opportunities, and then you can order up the opportunity you want. This concept, that we must activate capabilities within the subconscious before we use them, is not mentioned in any other resource I have found. If you do not believe that the subconscious is capable of X, then it will not be, and your requests for X will fail. That is how powerful our minds are. Our thoughts and beliefs shape everything in our existence, including the abilities of our own minds.

Chapter Two - Using Conscious Thought In A Definitely Creative Manner

The subjective mind is exactly what the name implies; it is a subject or a servant of the conscious mind of man. It is a servant in the sense that it was created for the use of man. It is entirely at his disposal. All that a man has to do is to command. The subconscious always obeys.

It obeys order whether consciously or unconsciously given. It is of so sensitive a nature, that every thought registers upon it. The conscious mind is the one and only force to which the subconscious mind responds. Conscious thought has power.

The human concept of power is physical. Power, in reality, is a product of mind. Mind, in all its different phases, is God. Mind is spirit. God is spirit. Man is spirit. Recognizing the unity of all and claiming this unity for himself, establishes for man contact with divinity. Man said, "There is one source from which all things come. The source is God. God is spirit. God is mind. I am one with the spirit and mind of God."

Power is the term by which energy is known to man. Thought energy is the greatest form of energy that exists, for back of thought is mind, and although mind is back of everything that exists, thought is more closely allied to mind than is any other form of energy. That, in a brief manner, explains why thought has power.

Concentrated thought is more powerful than idle thought. In order for the thoughts of man to make a definite impression upon the subconscious mind, they must be of sufficient force to register. By force, I mean intensity. Intensity is achieved by concentration. In order to concentrate, stillness and a certain amount of quietude are necessary. That is why you hear so much about the silence. It is necessary for effective work.

There is nothing mysterious about going into the silence. It is simply to allow the mind to gather its forces and focus them upon the sensitive plate or negative, to use a photographic term, of the subconscious mind. In concentration, a man causes his thought force to come to a focus or central point, and at this point there is a concentration of energy. This can be explained by the illustration of a magnifying glass and the focus it can make of the rays of the sun. It is the difference between scattered vibrations and the vibrations which radiate from a focal point. Just as the sun's rays gain in intensity and are able to burn when focused upon a certain place, in like manner, thought vibrations which are in many respects similar to the rays of the sun, gain a similar intensity. They make not only a definite, but a lasting impression upon the subconscious mind.

The conscious mind of man is the human dynamo that sends power to the subconscious mind. It is this dynamic quality which a man should employ to do creative work, and since the conscious mind is the only force to which the subconscious responds, a man should understand the manner in which the conscious mind should be used.

The method should be as follows: first, stillness, then quiet. These are simply to prevent extraneous matters from interfering with the idea which the individual wishes to hold. This idea or thought should embody several things. There first must be a desire, and the more overwhelming the desire the more definite the impression upon the subconscious mind. Desire is, in reality, a form of prayer, if a man realizes that God is the source of universal supply.

After the desire, there must be a realization that God's bounty is ever at mankind's disposal. It is this realization that I shall often refer to as acceptance. It is a mental acceptance and it is what is meant by the words, "What things soever ye desire when ye pray, believe that you have them and you shall have them." First is desire, then acceptance.

Realization of these first two requisites is essential, for they constitute the basis upon which rests the entire process. After these two things are firmly established in the conscious mind, the rest is easy. A man should next concentrate upon the thing which he desires. The manner of concentration is this: he should sit quietly and begin to see, in his mind, the thing which he wants.

For example, a man wishes to earn a definite sum of money for a specific purpose. First, he should concentrate upon that sum of money. He should see himself in possession of that amount; either in gold, silver, currency or a check made out to himself. He should hold that picture in his mind for a few moments. He may elaborate the picture in any manner he may choose. He can take the money and open a purse and put it inside. He can see himself depositing it in a bank, that is, giving it to a cashier or doing anything he feels inclined to do. The more earnestly he throws himself into the picture, the more effectually will the picture take hold. Then he should see himself using this same money to purchase or to pay off the thing he had in mind.

If it is an automobile, to illustrate, he should see himself going to the showroom. He should see himself going through the identical process that he would go through if he were actually buying a car. He can order it delivered or he can get into it and drive it home. After forming the complete picture, the next thing is to claim this thing for his own, calling himself by name. He then says, "I command the power inherent within me to hold this thought in mental concentration until it is manifested to me."

If he does this with enough conviction that he can do these things, and makes the mental picture consistently, and keeps it up long enough, the idea or thought will be impressed upon the universal mind through his subjective mind, until a manifestation is brought into existence. By existence, I mean into his physical possession.

Suppose a man owes money; his home is mortgaged. He has no manner of raising the money to meet the mortgage. The main thing to do is to stop worrying; that forms a positive blocking of the creative process. He should use his will power and hold in his conscious mind a picture of the house belonging to him free from all encumbrance. The same picture will register upon the subconscious mind and the power inherent within himself will cause to be manifested sufficient funds to meet the indebtedness. He should say to himself daily, "I am in touch with a power that knows all things. That is all the power that exists. This power is available to me whether I understand it or not. It is in operation at all times, whether I use it or not. It can provide me with everything I need, if I call upon it. I now decree for myself the money necessary to meet my every need. The house is now free from encumbrance in the realm of the universal, and what exists in the realm of the universal must manifest in the realm of the material."

He should not concern himself with the manner in which these things are to be brought to him. He should do whatever comes his way and affirm that divine mind knows the things necessary for the fulfillment of the things he wants. Man must have the conviction that he has a power inherent within himself to make a visualization come into manifestation or he is only wasting his time. There must be an absolute conviction that it is coming to him by virtue of his God-given power to do constructive work with his mind.

Just to sit idly and imagine a thing he would like to possess, will not bring them to him. The idea itself does not do creative work, unless there is a strong motive power of thought back of it. Otherwise, all that a person would have to do would be to wish for something. The chief thing to do is to think clearly, to the exclusion of everything else. Then he should take several minutes to let the picture register upon his subconscious mind.

Often, a person desiring a thing with such an overwhelming desire that he unconsciously forms a mental picture and it manifests in a manner approaching a thing which he desires. The thought, in a sense, manifests, yet it does not manifest of itself alone. The thought always makes an impression upon the subconscious. The subconscious imparts this impression to the great universal. The universal always responds. That is the reason why certain people succeed and why others fail.

Certain people know exactly what they want. The subconscious is then able to carry out their ideas because their minds have a definite concept of the thing they want accomplished. I am telling you this in an order that you may understand the importance of making definite plans. Get a definite mental picture of the thing you desire.

I have stated before, that there is a great deal of difference between idle thinking and constructive thinking. Constructive thinking means this: it is knowing that there is an inherent power within man that enables him to use his power of thought to bring into manifestation the thing which he wants. I say "wants," for man is not supposed to live by bread alone. Man may want things that he does not actually need. That is alright. God has filled the earth with limitless wealth. It was placed upon and under the earth for mankind's enjoyment.

A man should take time each day to decide upon or make definite statements about what he wants to happen. The words are not so important as the certainty within himself that he has the power and God given right to demand whatever he wants or needs. After a man has decided upon what he wants, he should make a mental picture of having that thing in his possession. Mental pictures always manifest. The reason for this is it gives the subconscious something definite to work upon.

A picture made by the conscious mind leaves what might be called a negative upon the subconscious mind, and I think that I shall say that a manifestation is simply a development of that negative. That is a term used in photography, and is a perfect illustration of the manner in which the conscious mind affects the subconscious mind. To complete the metaphor, the conscious mind is the camera. The subconscious is the plate upon which the negative is registered. The universal is the pool of liquid in which the negative is immersed, and it is of such a nature that it not only develops a picture but it also sends the same picture back to the photographer in a material form.

Concentration is necessary. Concentration is the act whereby a mental picture is focused into or through the camera, onto the plate of the subconscious, upon which a negative is registered. The chief thing to remember, in this connection, is that the subconscious mind requires what is called in photographic parlance a time exposure. The longer the time and the more concentrated the thought, the more perfect is the picture and the more successful will be the materialization.

An individual is conscious of his conscious mind. He cannot see it, but he knows that he possesses one. He is conscious of himself. It is this self-knowingness that makes him an individual. Although he cannot see his conscious mind, he accepts the fact without question that he has one. But he does not always accept the fact that he has a subconscious mind, because he is not conscious of it to the same degree that he is of his conscious mind. The subconscious mind of man is as much a reality as is his conscious mind.

Consider that the conscious mind and the subconscious mind are realities; that a proper understanding of the relation the one bears to the other may be the means of supplying mankind's every need. Man has but to seek and he will find whatever he seeks, whether it be health, wealth or illumination or any kind whatsoever.

Notes

In this chapter, we see the process in detail:

1. *Be still*
2. *Be in silence*
3. *Feel desire*
4. *Feel acceptance*
5. *Visualize what you want*
6. *Let it go*

This method is a little different than modern methods in that the acceptance of what you want comes BEFORE you visualize it. Here, acceptance is more general. You are training the mind to accept what you desire, in an overarching sense, and you are further embedding the belief that it will all come to you. And therefore it will. I like this method of training yourself to accept or receive in the general sense, rather than working to receive or accept each particular request.

If the practice of acceptance or receiving is not working for you, try releasing resistance instead. In my own practice, I have found that a daily focus on releasing resistance produces quick results. Acceptance and receiving are our natural state, but we often build up resistance in our minds, bodies and energies. We block ourselves like placing big rocks in a river. Remove the rocks, and the river flows naturally.

Chapter Three - Success, Failure

If the idea of success is established with sufficient conviction in the conscious mind of an individual, it not only makes success possible, it makes failure impossible. The idea of success contains within itself the essential elements of success, and it will, in time, attract to the individual whatever is necessary to enable him to attain success in some line of endeavor.

It is far better for the individual if he holds in his mind definite plans or ideas that is an ambition to succeed in some particular line of endeavor. However, even that is not necessary. If there is present in the individual an overwhelming desire to succeed in something or anything, the field may be left wide open, if the individual has no special talent or if he has received no training along a particular line of endeavor.

The universal possesses an infallible sense of discrimination, and if the individual calls upon it to attract to him something that is in line with his innate talent or abilities, the universe will immediately respond. It sets in operation certain forces that contain within themselves the power to attract to the individual of things that will make possible his success.

There is dormant in each human being, a faculty, whether it is developed or not, which will enable that particular individual to succeed, if the desire for success is present in his conscious mind. The conscious mind alone has the power of self-expression or desire and the entire subjective realm of mind is at the disposal of the conscious mind of man. I make this statement in order to emphasize the fact that man has the power and the right - the God-given right to use the subjective mind, both individual and universal, to attract to himself the things necessary for his happiness and success.

The conscious mind of man should accept the fact that man has an innate creative power. Man should develop a conscious conviction of this fact. When a man doubts his own power or ability to overcome obstacles, he should realize that the back of his own mind is divine mind, and when he has convinced himself that this divine power is available to him, and that he can make and is actually making use of it, doubt and fear automatically disappear.

Lack

The reason that any man lacks anything in his life is simply due to what might be termed a negation. The thought of an individual is able to attract to him the thing that thought embodies. The thought of lack contains within itself the elements that attract lack. The reason that lack exists in the experience of mankind is due to the fact that mankind has caused the idea of lack to be established in the universal subjectivity. Mankind alone is responsible for this idea, and now that it is established in the universal, if a man believes that it is a possibility, the universal accepts that belief as that man's desire and hence it becomes, in the universal, that man's decree. The result is that the universal sends lack to the individual who believes in lack.

It is simply the materialization of an idea. The universal responds to effort but the individual should reach out and grasp, with the tentacles of his mind, the things which he desires. There must be a conscious demand of the individual that the universe will deliver to him the things that he wants. The universal is indifferent, and it takes conscious effort on the part of the individual to establish definite thought vibrations or ideas in the universal.

The universal is of such a nature that it cannot care what it sends to the individual. It is sensitive, but not selective. It sends lack, which is only a minus sign, and it sends plenty, which is a plus. Lack, in reality, is a negative thing. It is only an absence of supply.

It is like a problem in mathematics, and that applies to the entire subject matter embodied in this book. If anyone is of sufficient intelligence to add and subtract, he can acquire the ability to cause to be manifested for him whatever he decrees in life. Perhaps I should state that all that is necessary for the individual to learn is the value of addition, and the subtraction problems will take care of themselves. That means, if the individual will only accept the statement that all that is necessary for him to do is to add, he can create for himself whatever he desires. Negative thoughts manifest as lack. Positive thoughts manifest as plenty.

Overcoming Circumstances

There exist certain conditions in the life of each individual, and to a certain extent those conditions are a dominating factor in the life of that individual. There are times when an individual seems to be, what the world terms, a victim of circumstance. Well, that is often true and it is due to the idea that exists in the mind of the individual that man is subject to conditions. By conditions, I mean circumstance and environment.

As a matter of fact, man is not subject to anything unless he himself permits himself to become a subject. There are no conditions, as the world understands conditions, in the universal subjectivity. It is what might be termed the absolute. Each thing is complete within itself in the universal. Nothing is related to anything else to such a degree that it must draw from something else or deprive anything else of anything in order to be self-existent. That is what I mean by the word absolute.

That same degree of self-expression is possible for any individual on earth, if the individual only realizes that fact. Each individual life should be complete within itself. It is possible for each individual to have perfect self-expression, if he is willing to overcome the idea of lack which exists in his conscious mind.

In order to overcome this idea, the individual may use a process of reasoning called the argumentative method. This method requires the assembling of certain facts in such a logical sequence, that the conscious mind accepts, beyond the possibility of doubt, certain propositions as true. It then becomes possible for the individual to establish a positive mental attitude in regard to them.

If a man has been holding thoughts of failure, poverty or lack, he may go through a mental process something like this. He should start with the realization that the thought of poverty or lack is powerless to influence his life or affect his affairs. If he denies that it has any power, he can then say, "This poverty in my life is the result of a mental concept. I have held in mind the idea of lack and that is all that has caused poverty to manifest in my affairs. I now deny that there is any idea of poverty in my mind, and I deny that there is any lack in universal mind. What appears to be poverty in my life is simply an absence of plenty. There is, in reality, no lack of anything in the universe. I alone have the power to decree lack for myself. This law was, in reality, caused by a belief that lack exists. This belief was an erroneous belief. I now realize that there is no lack, and that what appeared to be lack in my life, was due to this belief, which caused an absence of supply. God's substance is all about me, that I have the power to cause it to manifest in any form or manner, readily. The universal is always ready to respond to my decree, and I now decree for myself these things that divine mind has decreed that I may call into existence. And I now command the power inherent within me to hold in mental concentration these things until they are manifested for me."

The man should then name the things he has in mind and see each thing in his possession. After the realization of man's inherent power and right to use his creative faculties is established in his conscious mind, the foregoing process should not be necessary. As a man advances or develops the right degree of understanding, the conscious mind should act automatically in giving instructions to the subconscious. That is, the truth should become established in the conscious mind to such a degree that it should be unnecessary to go through the process of an argument to convince the conscious mind that certain adverse conditions have no power to interfere in the life of the individual.

If the individual can establish in his conscious mind a conviction of success, rather than fear of failure, adverse conditions can be completely destroyed. This is due to the fact that the subconscious mind must, at all times, adapt as its own whatever idea the conscious mind may be holding. The conscious mind has but to establish within itself the idea of success, and failure automatically disappears.

Notes

In this chapter, we see a quick note on something that I think needs a bit more emphasis: that any request that involves your innate gifts, talents, abilities, and therefore your life purpose, will be immediately granted. Some requests take time, but requests in support of your life purpose are granted NOW. Other requests may not be granted for some time, if it is counter to your purpose or otherwise not in your best interests. Ultimately, you get what you ask for, but sometimes I have noticed that the divine delays requests that are not a good choice for you. It is as if the divine is hoping you'll change your mind.

When it comes to lack versus abundance, these general concepts have profound effects on our daily lives. The most effective affirmation I have found to reprogram your mind towards abundance is from authors Mark Victor Hansen, and Robert G. Allen who said, "The Universe is fundamentally abundant."

In the section on overcoming circumstances, we see another key Hermetic concept: that you are under no obligation to participate in ANY circumstance, even if others may choose to do so. For example, some may choose health problems, financial lack, social hardships, inflation, abuse or any number of unpleasant situations. You do not have to participate.

For example, the entire world can choose to experience a pandemic, but you do not have to participate in their choice. You are not denying their choice to them. They get to choose whatever they like, and so do you. You are not begrudging them their choice to soak in fear, obsess over headlines, get really sick, suffer and grieve. Their choices are to be respected.

Not participating, in that example, means deciding deep down in your subconscious that you will not soak in fear, obsess over headlines, or otherwise allow anything to get in the way of your personal joy of living. You do the things that you love to do, and for anything you would like to do that no longer exists, you find another way.

You are not denying the reality of other people's choices. They have chosen it. You are respecting that this is what they want to experience right now. But you are just not going to participate. You are not going to be affected by other people's choices.

It can be a fruitful and fun exercise to list out all the things that society at large has chosen, and to decide which of those you do not choose to participate in. Watch your internal reaction when you choose. Is something in you working against you? Is something in you doubting that you can bow out of that experience? Are you blocking yourself? Work on clearing out the doubt, and choosing the circumstances that you will and will not participate in or experience.

Chapter Four - Effects Of Mental Attitude Of The Conscious Mind Upon The Subconscious

This topic refers solely to the varying emotions of the individual, not to his natural or normal mental attributes. The subconscious mind is so closely allied to the conscious mind, that it is one with it and at the same time it functions as a distinct entity. This functioning is of such an involved nature, that it would be impossible to take up that phase of the subconscious in detail, in this topic which you have asked me to discuss. However, I shall be able to explain briefly why the thoughts of the conscious mind affect the subconscious mind.

The subconscious mind, because it is the essence of mind, because it is powerless to have any self-expression, and because God has decreed that it is subjective to the conscious mind, is compelled to take not only the mental or intellectual attributes of the conscious mind, but the varying emotions as well. These varying emotional attitudes have a decided effect upon the creative process in the subjective realm.

Since the subconscious mind acts only under the direction of the conscious mind, and since the subconscious mind is the medium by which man attracts to himself the things held in abstraction in the universal, it follows that if an individual holds the thought that something is going to happen to him, he actually attracts that thing to him, whether it be good or bad. I use the word "bad" as it is considered the opposite of "good". As I shall repeat often, good is of a positive nature. Evil of any kind, is purely of a negative nature. It is a form of mental darkness; a lack of understanding. It may be called a form of ignorance or unenlightenment.

The light of understanding dispels ignorance, in like manner, good destroys evil. Bear that in mind. I should like at some future time to go into this in a more comprehensive manner. Each thought that a man thinks has its own quality or mental atmosphere. It produces a certain mental reaction. There are varying degrees of mental reactions and each mental attitude - sorrow, joy, misery, happiness, love, hate, interest, indifference - has its own mental reaction or vibration.

The person who habitually maintains a feeling of hope, expectancy and desire has a far better chance, let us say for success, than a person who is morbid and despondent. Those first name attributes are contributing factors but they are not sufficient in themselves to establish success. In reality, it is the sum total of a man's mental attitudes as well as mental attributes that make his life a success or a failure.

This is so involved a process, it will require a volume to explain the manner in which mental attitudes affect a person's life. Suffice it to say that the vibration of an individual determines what he shall experience in life, and that these vibrations are determined solely by the thoughts which an individual has stored up in his subconscious mind.

So for the present, let us stop and merely consider the fact that a person has the power to determine what his mental vibrations may be in the future, regardless of what they may have been in the past. In this manner he may be able to change conditions in his life, if he so decides. Thought tendencies are sometimes innate within a man, but regardless of how he may have come to certain mental attributes or attitudes, he has the God-given power to determine for himself what things or experiences may come to him.

Thoughts originate in the conscious mind of man, and those thoughts are the determining factor. The subconscious mind is a receiving station, and it is the storehouse of every thought which a man has ever had. It is not only memory, it is a powerhouse from which emanates constantly a flow or stream of messages in the form of mental pictures to that source of unlimited supply which is called universal subjectivity.

The universal subjectivity might be likened to an immense manufacturing plant where every known product is created.

From that great manufacturing plant comes everything that is in the visible universe. Remember that each individual has sent, and is eternally sending, either consciously or unconsciously, orders to the universal plant. Remember that the universal ever sends to the individual the sum total of his order. By some total, I mean this: If the individual sends out an order with mixed feelings of hope and despondency, happiness and misery, positive and negative thoughts, his order is simply a hodgepodge of all these things, and in like proportions does he receive such things or conditions in his life and experience.

Thoughts are a form of energy. They determine the kind of material which the universal uses in making the things a man receives, or the conditions which enter into his life and experience. That is why it is necessary to guard the portals of the conscious mind. Keep the door shut to thoughts of sickness, disease and disaster. Open a door to thoughts of health, plenty and prosperity. These things can enter the subconscious mind only through the conscious mind.

The subconscious mind is the only medium by which the individual may contact the universal source of supply. The subconscious mind does not choose, nor has it the power to reject. It simply accepts whatever the conscious mind decrees.

Notes

In this chapter, we see that thoughts have emotions associated with them, and that both thoughts and emotions are taken in by the subconscious mind. Further, whatever mix of thoughts and emotions that we send (even if we didn't mean to send it), comes back to affect our lives by bringing us more of that exact same mix. So we must be very careful to guard our thoughts AND our emotions.

When this book was first written, avoiding other people's thoughts was relatively easy. You could choose the company you keep and you could avoid newspapers and radio news. Today, avoiding other people's thoughts and emotions means avoiding not just headlines, and negative people, but avoiding all social media and other online content. It means being something of a digital hermit.

Everything you read, listen to, watch, observe, everyone you talk to and are near to, and every little post that anyone sneaks into your awareness are placing thoughts and emotions into your conscious mind and therefore into your subconscious mind. That means that every post you look at, every video you watch, and every headline you read is crafting your reality, based on someone else's choices, thoughts and emotions. Tread carefully.

The revelation that the subconscious stores everything you ever put into it should be cause for some serious consideration. That means all the inadvertent requests for negative experiences that you piled up in the subconscious, and all the times prior to your awakening that you were angry, fearful, sad, or otherwise sending signals of negativity or lack into your subconscious mind, are still on record to be fulfilled.

To counter all of that, I recommend that the first time you choose to take conscious control of the subconscious mind, you might choose to clear its memory and start with a blank slate. Because the subconscious can do exactly what we declare it can do, you might declare that it clear out its memory and start fresh.

Chapter Five - Fear

Fear drives success away from humanity. It even causes utter annihilation. It carries poverty and defeat in its path. It raises the barrier to divine response. Fear is doubt. Doubt is the result of a lack of understanding that God is mankind's supply. Fear is a belief in limitation, and it even causes that condition to manifest in the life and experience of the one who believes in limitation. By limitation, I mean that condition in the experience of mankind whereby he is not provided with the things he desires.

Divine mind is the source of all that there is. That means that God has so arranged conditions that it is possible for mankind, through established contact with him, to be provided with all things. This contact is established by first acknowledging that God is all there is; that he is in everything, that man is one with God, that god is man's supply, and by a mental acceptance of the bounty of God. Fear is a belief that things are being withheld.

The truth is that man has already received all things needed, but they are in the abstract and man must desire to call them into manifestation. The desire must come first, but that is not enough of itself. Man must also recognize the fact that he must use the power that God has placed within mankind in order to cause the things which he wants to manifest to him.

This power is placed in man in order that man may have a part in the creation of the things he desires. The process is a mental one, and really is the same process which God himself uses in the creation of the universe. It is, in a manner, a contemplation of the things that man wishes to have appear or come into his experience.

This process requires effort on the part of man. It is not idle thinking, but a definite and positive concept of the thing which he wants. The process requires concentration. It also requires a greater degree of understanding than is possessed by a person who has not developed along mental and spiritual lines. This understanding and growth come with study of the teaching of those who have acquired knowledge of the truth that all is governed by law and it can be attained by all mankind.

To revert to the original statement that fear blocks or hinders the divine response; fear is a belief in an adverse power. In reality, there is no adverse power. Divine mind is all the power there is. Fear is mental and affects the mental process in the subconscious. The subconscious is the medium whereby everything which relates to mankind's needs can be provided or brought into manifestation.

The conscious mind of man is a determining factor in the creative process. It gives orders, which the subconscious mind is compelled to obey. These orders are not necessarily consciously given. The subconscious is so subtle that it reacts with a greater degree of sensitiveness than man can conceive. It takes on the man's vibrations and these vibrations are, in reality, the determining factor.

God has caused to exist certain vibrations. These vibrations are a form of energy. The degree of vibrations differ in every element. The rate of vibrations, or the degree of energy which anything possesses, determines the character of that particular thing. Each individual has his own vibration. This vibration determines what he attracts to himself. Thoughts determine vibrations, and as a man's thoughts change, in like manner do his vibrations change. They are determined by his mental reaction. If he is happy, his vibrations are of a certain degree, if he is angry, they are of a different degree, and for every mental condition there is a corresponding vibration. Faith has a vibration that is endowed with a peculiar power of attraction. It has a drawing power that is not possessed by any other vibration. That is why faith is necessary to attract to mankind to things which he wants.

Even a man who has no understanding of the law can attract things to himself if he is a type that believes in his own ability. His vibrations are of a degree that approach faith vibrations. He is convinced of his power to such an extent that his vibrations are sufficiently powerful to overcome doubt.

Fear has a vibration that interferes with other vibrations. It is very powerful, for it causes a confusion in the conscious mind that is reflected into the subjective mind, and the subjective mind becomes confused in turn and its vibrations waver. The vibrations of the subconscious lose contact with the vibrations in the universal reservoir. The power of attraction is destroyed. The things that may have been started or directed in the reservoir toward the individual are discontinued. They may retain a certain energy or cohesion for a while, but if the fear vibrations continue in that person, the elements that are being drawn together in the abstract are eventually dissolved into their original condition. That is why fear is destructive.

Notes

In this chapter, we learn that fear is lack and limitation in disguise. That's another good reason to let fear go. And that would be enough, but we also learn that emotions have distinct vibrations.

This is an idea that has rippled through various authors' work from Joe Dispenza to The Secret, and just about every other teacher discussing manifestation. It is an extension of the idea that everything has vibration. Therefore, thoughts and emotions have vibrations too. Fear has a vibration that disrupts the process. Whatever you are trying to manifest in your life, fear will prevent it.

This is counter to the concept seen in some other works, such as Existential Kink by Carolyn Elliott, PhD, which suggests that fear and desire are the same thing. Therefore, fearing something will bring it to you just as much as desiring it. In my own practice, what looks like fear in the conscious mind is sometimes carefully disguised desire. We might desire something socially unacceptable such as desiring illness or poverty, and so the conscious mind disguises it as a fear we can't stop talking about, which is more acceptable.

It takes a deep awareness of your truth to see what is actually fear and what is desire masquerading as fear. In the end, if it is really desire, you will receive what you are seeking. If it really is fear, you will not receive anything at all, even the things you really did want. One way to tell the difference is to look around you. If you have something in your life that you claim you don't want, or that you claim you fear, you need to dig deeper. It is in your life because you requested it. It is worth the effort to figure out why so you can let it go.

The discussion of faith as the highest vibration is unique. In Joe Dispenza's work we see emotions like love and gratitude as the highest vibrations. Faith, here, is framed as an emotion or an emotional thought. This makes sense if we think of faith as the combination of desire and acceptance or receiving that was key to the process.

Either way, emotions carry a lot of weight with the subconscious mind. While visualizing your desires, it helps to feel what it would be like to have them already. Infusing the visualization with positive emotion helps the process. Another strategy is to request a life that feels a certain way, and leave the details up to the divine. For example, you might request a life that feels exciting, or joyous, or fun, or abundant-joy-fun and see what comes.

Chapter Six - Health

In order to understand what sickness is, it is necessary to understand what health is. Health is the natural condition of mankind. Disease is simply a distortion of the natural condition of man. Disease is a negative condition. Health is a positive condition. That you can understand, as nature constantly strives to establish health in any disease.

The first state of mankind is one of perfection. Man is an expression of divine mind and divine mind creates only perfect things. It follows that only perfection should be manifested. Health is the idea of man which is at all times held in divine mind. The divine idea of man is a perfect idea. Disease is only the idea, or faulty idea, which mankind himself has caused to be manifested in the life of man.

Man alone is responsible for imperfect conditions in his life. Perhaps that statement should be elaborated. I wish to remind you that God has given man the power to work independently of him. Man has been given the power to change conditions. He has the power to accept or to reject. He has permitted negative conditions to be manifested. He has permitted negative thoughts to predominate. Universal mind has accepted this predominance of negative thoughts as mankind's decree and confusion is the result.

Not until man himself decrees perfect adjustment, can perfect adjustment take place in his life and experience. This perfect adjustment in his physical body, man has the inherent power to decree by conscious thought. The reason that people become ill is that the idea of illness has, at some time, been impressed upon the subconscious mind of the individual.

This need not be done to the conscious thought of the individual. It may be due to thought transference. An impression is made upon the individual's subconscious mind by contacting the ideas sent out into the universal subjectivity by the subconscious mind of individuals who believe in sickness and disease.

The universal mind is the medium of thought transference. It is, at first, the conscious thought of one individual. That individual's mind takes hold of or seizes upon the thought and it vibrates that thought to the universal subjectivity. The universal subjectivity transfers that thought vibration to the subconscious mind of certain individuals whose subconscious minds are receptive to that thought.

If the conscious mind of an individual is opposed to that thought, it can make no impression upon the subconscious mind of that particular individual. He is immune to the idea. Not even the universal mind can implant a thought upon the mind of the individual who opposes the idea back of the thought. In view of this fact, it is easily understood why certain people are well and remain well through certain epidemics.

The reason that conscious mind can cure disease is this: the body is a product of mind. The subconscious mind is the builder of the body. The power of the conscious mind is supreme over the subconscious mind. For this reason, the conscious mind is able to change any idea that the subconscious mind holds.

This can be done by commanding the subconscious to substitute another idea in place of any particular idea which the subconsciousness may be holding. It is not difficult to impress the idea of health upon the individual's subconscious mind if the conscious mind is convinced that it can be done. An absolute conviction is essential. Unless this conviction is present, the subconscious is so sensitive to thought that it realizes the doubt.

Disease is negative. Negative thoughts are responsible for disease. Positive force or energy overcomes negative energy. Substitute the word thought for the word energy and you have the reason why it is possible to overcome illness of whatsoever nature. Make a conscious demand that the subconscious substitute the idea of health for the idea of disease.

This may be done by a denial of disease in general or in particular. Once the idea of disease is eliminated, it is easy to replace it with the idea of health. Sometimes it helps to make a statement in regard to the particular defect or weakness. Denials serve to eradicate ideas. Affirmative statements serve to establish definite ideas in the subconscious mind.

One certain way to impress the subconscious is to make a mental picture. If an organ is weak and fails to function as it should, the individual should visualize himself as doing the things he would be doing if he were in perfect health. If the realization back of any statement is one of deep conviction, it will in time cause the subconscious mind to build or rebuild the body in accordance with the idea back of it.

A man may say, "God is the source of all there is. The life of God is all the life there is. I am one with the life of God. God is too perfect to create imperfection, and as a manifestation of divine mind, I am, in reality, perfect. That perfection is now being substituted for imperfection. Health is now replacing sickness. The only image which has ever been in divine mind is a perfect image, and I now command the power within me to form my body in perfect duplication of the perfect image held in divine mind."

Divine mind is of a positive nature. It has within itself negative and positive energy. It uses these two opposites for the purpose of achieving contrast, but not in a manner in which man understands. Negative energy is one of the means by which divine mind regulates power. If there were no means by which energy could be regulated, there would be no degrees of power. Divine mind uses negative energy constructively, not destructively.

Not even the universal mind has the power to regulate energy. It understands the method of using it after it is regulated, but only the mind of God himself has a supreme intelligence and power to regulate energy.

The negative portion of energy and the positive portion of energy are known to man in the use he makes of electricity. In times past, electricity was unknown. Now that man understands electrical energy, it should assist him to understand or realize that there are degrees of energy of which mankind is ignorant.

One of these degrees of energy is the energy of thought. Thought is mental force. It is the highest type of energy. Thought force is as definite a force as is the physical force with which man is familiar. It is of so much greater energy that there is no comparison.

Physical force is, in reality, the weakest form of energy known. It is the force of matter and matter is the dust of energy. That term "dust" is a comparative word. It is used to convey the lightest substance with which you are familiar.

Thought is initial energy. Thoughts are direct products of mind, and back of the mind of man is the mind of God. The conscious mind of man is a portion of one of the degrees of the conscious mind of God. It is this conscious mind that enables man to have the power of self-expression. For this reason, man was allowed to use negative and positive energy. The proper use requires that a definite balance be established. When there is not enough positive energy, there is a lack of energy.

Divine mind arranged things in a perfect balance. Either through a lack of understanding or a misconception of things, man has disturbed the perfect balance and has not yet re-established. Confusion and adverse conditions are the results. It remains for man to re-establish this perfect balance, and the easiest manner by which this can be done is to establish contact with divine mind.

A man can, by prayer, establish such a perfect contact with divine mind that automatically the perfect equilibrium or balance of negative and positive energy is established for him. That is why the prayer of faith is effective, without any conception of the why.

God is ever ready to respond to the appeal of mankind, whether it is a supplication of faith or whether it is the result of mankind's realization that God is all, that God has established perfection, and that all man has to do is to accept the perfect conditions which God has already provided. The process is so simple that it is surprising that mankind has been so long in realizing how it can be done. God has established perfection in the universe, and this perfection is inherent within mankind.

The individual should establish the truth of the following words in his subconscious mind. "I am the expression of the perfect mind of God. This perfection is inherent within me. I now call into manifestation perfect harmony; perfect adjustment in mind and body. My body is but the expression of mind. My mind is one with the perfect mind of God. I am, in reality, perfect, regardless of appearance. I have been given the power to decree for myself perfect adjustment and I now decree for myself harmonious adjustment both in mind and body. I am now contacting the perfect order and harmony of divine mind. This harmony causes every adverse condition to disappear. I call upon divine mind to aid the power within me to hold in mental concentration the perfect image of me that is held at all times in divine mind."

Illness of any kind is weakness. If enough energy is called into expression, the disease must disappear of itself. Disease is, in reality, a lack of energy. Disease is a negative condition. It disappears if the individual can call into expression sufficient energy, which overcomes lack of any kind. That is why rest is so often beneficial. It gives the energy time to flow in.

If an individual only realized it, he would cause energy to flow in at will or even to flow in such a continuous stream that there would never be a lack. A man should say, "The eternal energy of divine mind is ever flowing into my mind and body and I am strengthened each moment. This energy is the source of my strength and health. Its healing power is now establishing perfect harmony and that harmony is now manifesting itself as perfect health."

Notes

The explanation of transference is possibly the best I have seen. Every human being on the earth is sending ideas into the universal subconscious or divine subconscious. Those ideas are then downloaded into the minds of anyone who might be open to them. This is the mechanism, that draws the right people to bring you the experiences you requested. But it's also a back door through which the collective human consciousness can effectively subvert your subconscious requests. In the next chapter, we see a discussion of how to protect ourselves from that effect.

The discussion of thoughts as energy, and disease as caused by negative thoughts or as a lack of energy, feels familiar. In Reiki, Qigong, and other forms of energy work, disease is treated through the addition of energy into the body, and the clearing of energy blocks. Negative thoughts or emotions drain energy from the body, leading to disease. The state of our energy ultimately affects the body. So here we see that the mind leads the energy, which leads the body. If you fix the mind, you will fix the energy, and therefore fix the body.

Using negative energy constructively is a neat concept that is unique to this book. In my own practice, I can see several ways to do that. Not all negatives are bad. You might choose to lack things like fear, enemies, or disease. Lack is a an idea based in negative energy. You might choose to experience destruction in order to create. For example, you might take apart a wooden pallet in order to build a side table. Or you might inject negative energy into the universal subconscious in order to disrupt or alter specific ideas being sent there by humanity at large. There is an ethics issue there to be addressed for sure, but the point stands. All the paint colors are useful in creating the masterpiece. Negative energy, appropriately applied, can be very constructive indeed.

Overall, this discussion of health drives home the critical larger concept that, "Man alone is responsible for imperfect conditions in his life." When we can face that we alone are responsible for the conditions in our lives, then we can take the authority to change those conditions any way we like. If you want the authority, and therefore the ability, you have to accept the responsibility. This is the single hardest thing to face, in my opinion, in the personal journey - that you, and only you, brought every experience to yourself - the good ones, the bad ones, and everything between.

Chapter Seven - Confidence In Self, Faith In God

Confidence is that condition of mind which is the result of a realization that nothing can prevent success in an undertaking. It is this feeling, more than any other, that is the contributing factor to the successful accomplishment of an idea. I say idea, for an idea is necessary before anything can be even so much as attempted.

Certain positive mental attitudes combine to constitute confidence. They are: assurance, a conviction of success, a determination that nothing shall prevent or interfere with achievement, and a certainty within the mind of the individual that he has innate power that can be called upon to overcome outside interference. The things which I have just enumerated are the attributes any normal man possesses. They are the natural endowment of an ordinary individual's conscious mind.

The conscious mind has the power to establish vibrations in the subconscious mind, which embodies the idea which the conscious mind holds. When an individual is of a definitely positive nature, he is able to establish vibrations in his subconscious mind which are of sufficient strength to reach far out into the universal and contact similar vibrations in the universal. The universal law of attraction is that like attracts like. Vibrations of one degree attract vibrations of a similar degree. It is because this law is an invariable and unchangeable law that man is able to attract to himself the things which he desires.

The same with which you are familiar, that we are begripped with spiritual laws which execute themselves, is a true statement. It means simply this: there are laws in the universe that are so powerful and so perfectly adjusted to each other, that all a man has to do is to start one of these laws to operate, and then the other laws are compelled by their own nature to fall in line with the requirements that are necessary to cause the perfect execution of the first law that began to operate.

An individual's vibrations, once established in a sufficiently positive manner, should maintain a continuous flow from his subconscious to the universal, if they are to be effective in attracting to the individual the thing he desires. Certain individuals are of an extremely positive nature. Others are inclined to be of a negative nature which, as I have explained elsewhere, is due to a lack of energy or force. If an individual of an extremely positive nature establishes vibrations in his subconscious mind, the subconsciousness is able to maintain these vibrations, owing to the fact that the conscious mind of the individual does not waver. The initial force, remember, is in the conscious mind.

If an individual who is of a slightly negative mentality sends his vibrations through his subconscious mind into the universal, it often happens that there is a cross-current of vibrations coming from a more positive individual. This cross current may not be of the same intensity or degree and if it is not, it will have no effect upon the slightly negative vibrations. But if the positive vibrations are of a similar degree, the vibrations of the negative quality will be deflected and oftentimes will be completely diverted in their flow into the universal. That is why at times a man's work is rendered null.

The two individuals may not even know each other, but if they are working to attain the same thing, then it is disastrous to the man who is sending out the less positive or slightly negative vibration. That is why it is necessary for an individual to adapt an absolutely positive attitude in regard to the things which he wishes to happen, attain, or require.

It is possible for a man to change from a negative to a positive nature and it is only by making this change that he is able to establish vibrations in his subconscious mind that will enable him to call forth from the universal the things which are necessary for his happiness.

In this topic, I have dealt with the conscious mind of the individual in its relation to a subconscious mind. The vibrations of the individual subconscious were explained and the conflict between these vibrations and the vibrations of the subconscious minds of more powerful individuals. I have tried to show that in the world of human affairs mankind is, to a certain extent, at the mercy of other individuals who possess a decidedly more positive nature. I have tried to explain why some people succeed and why others fail. I have shown that positive vibrations have the power to overcome, divert and intercept vibrations of a less positive degree, when the vibrations are of a similar intensity or the same degree.

There is a certain way, however, by which an individual may protect himself from all human interference. This I shall now discuss in the following topic.

Faith In God

Faith in God is the realization that there is in the universe a supreme power, ever present, all-wise, all-powerful, all-loving, all-protecting, all-providing and that this power is ever at the disposal of mankind, if he calls upon it. Man looks upon God as some vague, incomprehensible being or principle, or some intangible something in some distant realm. Divinity does reside in distant realms, but he is the very essence of man. He is in man's mind soul and body.

Man should strive to learn the fundamentals of this new manner of regarding his relation to God. Man will have to realize his oneness with the source of being.

God has decreed that man shall be able to control his life without divine interference. Divine mind does not resist man's desire, even though that desire is an unworthy one, but that does not mean that God has set mankind adrift.

The greatest contributing factor to success which a man possesses is an understanding that there is a power higher than human power, which is ever at his disposal. It is the feeling which may be described in the words, "underneath are the everlasting arms." That is one manner of referring to divinity and it imparts a feeling of security to the individual who has so far progressed in spiritual understanding that he realizes the truth of the words.

Faith in God, combined with the earnest efforts of an individual, will bring success at all times. Do not understand me to imply that all that a man should do is sit still and expect success to come to him without effort. Man should strive to develop the talents which God has conferred upon him. In order for a man to grow, it is necessary for him to develop his innate talent or ability, and this requires constant development of the faculties which he is endowed.

Only the individual himself has this power. It must come from man himself. Subjective mind ever waits upon man's demand. I use the word demand, for man has the right - the God-given right - to demand of subjective mind. It is but a portion of the mind of God, which he has set aside for the use of mankind. It must obey the decree of man's conscious mind.

When, however, the individual permits doubt or fear to encompass him about, there is no directing contact with the universal subjectivity. The contact is always present, but the universal receives no definite orders. The individual's subconscious receives no definite impression as to what he wishes brought to him, and the individual has no other means of imparting orders to the universal subjectivity.

Fear and doubt cause confusion in the conscious mind. That creates confusion in the subconscious mind and causes the vibrations to waver or even to break connection entirely. The result is that man is caught in the varying vibrations of any and all individuals with whom he may establish contact, and the result is either lack or disorder of some kind.

Faith in divine power causes an inflow of divine energy and this energy serves to stabilize the mentality of the person who believes in and relies upon divine power and divine protection. The individual who believes in the efficacy of prayer or who has the understanding that all that is necessary is for him to claim for himself divine protection, receives additional strength to the degree commensurate with his faith.

Faith serves as a stabilizer. It makes possible perfect adjustment in the universal. It causes an inflow of divine power. It establishes continuity of vibration, and this continuity is necessary if the vibrations are to reach to the universal supply. The subconscious mind can sense the process. From afar off there comes an inflow of vibrations of such great power that they completely enmesh the vibration of the individual's subconscious mind.

First, these vibrations flow into the nebulae, which hold in abstraction the invisible essence containing the necessary elements to cause to manifest the thing the individual wants. These vibrations then flow from the nebula-like formation, which is in the universal, to the subconscious mind of the individual. These vibrations become so interlocked with the vibrations of the individual, that no human being's vibration can divert them in the slightest degree. This contact is maintained as long as the individual continues to ask divine mind to protect.

If the individual continues to trust in divine power, the thing which he desires comes to him in some manner. The more perfect the mental concept he has of the thing, the more perfect will be its manifestation.

Confidence in divine power, in divine protection, in divine love; these things alone are enough to make a man invincible. No man can fail if, in addition to his own efforts, he relies upon divine aid.

Notes

In this final chapter, we see the key to avoiding negative influence from other individuals or humanity at large - oneness with the divine, and to simply request that exact protection.

Oneness with the divine is the harder part, so let's start there. Oneness is an aspect that occurs naturally once you experience Stage Ten on the Cycle of Human Development (See the book, Purna Asatti, for details). Some people come to oneness through psychedelic or other profound experiences. To get there, and stay there for extended periods of time, you need only work your way through the tasks associated with each stage. Psychedelics are optional. If you tackle the stages (and their associated tasks) in order, it goes fairly quickly. The truth is that however you get to oneness is worth the effort.

As for asking, it is just that simple. Remember that EVERY aspect of your existence is within your authority. If you want protection from the cross-currents of other people's thoughts, decide that you will be protected. It can be easy to forget that. Decide what your reality will be and follow divine guidance to make it happen. It really is all up to you. And the magnificent reality you create will ripple positive thoughts through humanity, for the good of all.

Questions, Answers And Additional Resources

Do you have questions about what you have read here? Go to KathrynColleen.com and send in your questions. Kathryn will answer you back as quickly as possible.

Also at KathrynColleen.com, you will find:

- Links to the full edition of the book, *Purna Asatti*, which includes specific exercises and how-to for each task plus art and poetry for a different perspective on each stage.

- The music album, *Purna Asatti - Music For Complete Connection*, that accompanies the book.

- The podcast, *On Life And Being Human*, where many of your questions may be answered.

- Other books, albums, essays and art by Kathryn Colleen.

- And more!

About The Editor

Dr. Amy "Kathryn Colleen" Messegee, PhD RMT is an American-born author, composer and artist better known for her foundational work: *Purna Asatti*, a process and practice that uses connection to self, others and every aspect of your life for managing challenges and accelerating self development.

Her summer job at 16 was doing scientific research at NASA. Before her 25th birthday she earned her Ph.D in Mathematics and was speaking to conferences on human reasoning and how to make the infinite finite. A hyper-polymath, her career has enjoyed a ride through…

• academia (as a professor of Mathematics),

• defense technology (as a Scientist, CTO, and DARPA Program Manager),

• online media (as founder of a business website and video podcast with a reach of 1.3 million),

• venture capital (advising VC firms on evaluating technologies and reading the founders for their true intent),

- private education (as founder of a local network of elite tutors and private instructors),

- and her current passion: global peace, human connection and energy work.

In each of these, the theme is always the same: aggregating seemingly unrelated perspectives to distill a new approach for accelerated results. She has published many books, hundreds of articles and papers, dozens of unique art pieces and released multiple music albums.

She is known for taking only four students each year but influences and leads thousands around the world in more than 70 countries through speaking, writing, music, art and podcasts.

She is a Reiki Master Practitioner/Teacher and is travel-proficient in nine languages which she is learning simultaneously.

See KathrynColleen.com for more information, books, articles, music, podcasts, and resources.